92   c.1
Di
O'REGAN
Neil Diamond

DATE DUE			
SEP 29 '76			
OCT 6 '76			
APR 9 '77			
MAY 13 '77			

NeilDiamond★

text   **Suzanne K. O'Regan**
illustrations   **John Keely**
design concept **Mark Landkamer**

published by   **Creative Education**
              Mankato, Minnesota

Published by Creative Educational Society, Inc.,
123 South Broad Street, Mankato, Minnesota 56001
Copyright © 1975 by Creative Educational Society, Inc. International
copyrights reserved in all countries.
No part of this book may be reproduced in any form without written permission
from the publisher. Printed in the United States.
Distributed by Childrens Press, 1224 West Van Buren Street, Chicago, Illinois 60607
Library of Congress Number: 75-22462   ISBN: 0-87191-464-6
Library of Congress Cataloging in Publication Data
O'Regan, Suzanne K.   Neil Diamond.
Bibliography: p.
1. Diamond, Neil.   I. Keely, John.   II. Title.
ML3930.D4507   784'.092'4 (B)   75-22462   ISBN 0-87191-464-6

Neil Diamond once wrote a song about a frog who dreamed of being a king and was fortunate enough to become one. The song, "I Am . . . I Said," could easily be the story of Neil's life.

A Frog

Neil identified closely with the frog in his song. He was such an awkward kid. His ears were too big, and his nose always seemed to be in the way. His arms and legs were too long for his body, making "lanky" and "stringbean" the only descriptions that seemed to fit him. He didn't go out with girls, didn't have many friends.

Neil spent his childhood on the move. During World War II, Neil's family moved to Cheyenne, Wyoming, and lived there for three years. Cowboys and guitar music made a vivid impression on shy Neil. His interest in music was sparked by watching Saturday afternoon Westerns in some forgotten movie house. "My heroes were the singing cowboys in the movies," Neil once said.

Neil and his family moved to Brooklyn where his father owned a series of unsuccessful dry goods shops. Each new store meant a move and a new neighborhood for the Diamonds. Neil had gone to nine schools by the time he finished grade school. He always felt like an outsider. It was a lonely, solitary existence; and it left a deep impression on Neil.

Neil would often spend his free time listening to the "top forty" at home or in his father's store. These hours of just listening to the radio further developed his interest in music.

It was this lonesome life that helped Neil Diamond become a musician. Music became a desperate release for all kinds of feelings he didn't understand. Neil offered a good description of his childhood when he gave an explanation of the song, "I Am . . . I Said": "When I speak of dreaming about being a king in 'I Am . . . I Said,' the king represents acceptance. I was never accepted as a kid. I always wanted to be something. That's why I took to writing so passionately. Songwriting was an outlet for a great deal of frustration. Writing songs finally gave me something of my own."

When Neil was sixteen, those dreams somehow became a reality. He bought a guitar for nine dollars, paid it off a dollar a week, and started taking lessons. He took the lessons for three weeks and learned his first chord progression. On the day he learned the progression, he wrote his first song and never took another lesson. He, had found part of himself. The guitar was the key to many of his locked-up feelings and dreams.

In high school Neil's music became a major part of his life. He established a pattern of sleeping a few hours during the early night and then writing throughout the quiet night.

During this time Neil also developed an interest in science and in fencing. He had become very much interested in biology and enjoyed working at a microscope. Fencing was a way for Neil to keep in shape, a sport which fit his personality. He had always felt out of place in team sports; but, in fencing, he was by himself. He quickly became one of the best fencers in his area.

Diamond entered New York University as a pre-med student on a fencing scholarship, but music was still his preoccupation. He went to college because he felt that it

was what he had to do. Since he liked science, he felt he should consider becoming a doctor, although he knew that he really wanted to become a songwriter.

Neil continued to write songs while he was going to college. Soon he also began performing as a way of getting his music played and heard. Those performances were a tremendous help, and Neil still remembers them. "I had a lot of time to learn the ropes. I knew that I was a songwriter and that I would always be a songwriter. I had something to hang onto and considered myself more fortunate than most of my contemporaries because of this fact."

With only a half year to go before graduation, Neil Diamond was offered a writing contract by Sunbeam Music, a music publishing company. The salary was $50 a week. He was only ten units short of a college degree, but he knew he wanted to write songs more than anything. As Neil once put it, "The minute the staff writing offer was made, I jumped at it without a moment's hesitation. I quit New York University — thrilled. Someone was actually paying me to write music. Man, I mean I *ran* from school to take that job."

Learning the Ropes

In the early 1960's, established publishing companies hired a roster of would-be composers because they wanted to take advantage of the new sound in pop music. Neil was only twenty years old when he went to work as a songwriter on "Tin-Pan Alley," a tattered street on the edge of Broadway in New York City, where most of the music publishers had their offices.

At first, Neil's job seemed wonderful to him. It meant good money for a while. If he sold a song, he'd have fifty or seventy-five dollars to live on. Besides, it was exciting to meet and work with other songwriters.

But there was no glory or future in the job. The writers were placed in cubicles next to each other and were ordered to turn out catchy, commercial material in huge quantities. Sometimes the songs were to be geared toward a certain performer, sometimes toward that week's "sound."

Neil often felt like a tailor, trying to make a song fit an unknown singer who was searching for the perfect song that would make a superstar. Yet Neil remained in the tiny square room, matching songs to voices, going nowhere. Some of the other writers enjoyed this type of work. But for Neil and for many others, the work was frustrating and unrewarding. Neil was unable to write music the way someone else wanted it. As a result, he was almost a complete failure for eight years. Because he couldn't develop an interest in this kind of writing or turn out as many songs as the companies wanted, Neil was fired from five different publishers.

After he had been fired from his fifth publishing job, he felt he was really at the bottom. Somehow he had to start climbing up. He either had to get out of the music business, or try writing on his own without the security of a weekly paycheck. He decided finally to try to make it on his own. He had to see for himself whether his ideas about

music were good or whether the publishers had been right in firing him. Neil rented a little storeroom above a nightclub for $35 a month and managed to find a used piano for fifteen dollars. The only other furnishing in the room was a pay phone.

Neil lived in that tiny little room for a year and began to write music for no one but himself. There were no more restrictions. There were no more producers, hanging over his shoulder, telling him to "throw in some bongos" or to "speed up the tempo." He wrote just what he felt, whether it was about life, love, or anger. Music became his entire life; and he wrote morning, noon, and night.

The challenges which Neil confronted in this tiny storeroom taught him two very important things. He learned that he was a good inventive composer and that he could sing well enough to make his own records. When his friends heard the demonstration records of his songs, they asked him why he wasn't performing. Their persuasion and Neil's desperation during this non-productive phase of his career convinced him to try performing. Then, he hoped, his music would be heard and accepted.

In 1964 he was booked into a Greenwich Village coffee house for a one-night stand and made an impression on record producers, Jeff Barry and Ellie Greenwich, who were in the audience. They signed him to a small, independent record label, Bang Records; and he began recording his own material. In fact, in his very first session, Neil recorded "Solitary Man." It became an immediate hit. Greenwich and Barry knew what to do. They knew what advice to give Neil and when to hold back and let him try his own ideas.

"Solitary Man" reflects the disappointments Neil had faced in his life. When it was first released, people kept asking Neil whether he actually was a "solitary man."

"Of course I was," he once remarked. "Anybody could see it — anybody but me."

Neil Diamond spent two years with Bang Records. He turned out such singles as "Cherry, Cherry," "I Got the Feeling," "Thank the Lord for the Night Time," and "Kentucky Woman." But Diamond still wasn't considered important enough to be able to decide for himself just which songs would be recorded. Bang Records was essentially a singles company, and he preferred albums. When Neil's contract expired, he left Bang to sign with Uni Records, a newly formed Universal Studios label. He hoped that at Uni he could concentrate his energies on the kind of musical ideas that were best developed in album form.

This change in record labels made an even bigger change in Neil Diamond's career. He stopped doing personal appearances at teen dances, bowling alleys, and gymnasiums.

Neil also made the difficult move from New York to California. He hated to leave New York. His roots were there, and he regarded it as home. Yet he knew that, for the sake of his career, he had to live in Los Angeles. He needed the contact with other musicians which would be hard to find in New York.

These changes gave Neil the chance to gain more control over his music. With no more financial pressure to do one-time local appearances, he had the chance to develop an album the way he wanted to do it. When it

14

came out, the album was called, *Velvet Gloves and Spit.* It was a failure. Some parts embarrassed even Neil, but it was a breakthrough. The experience allowed him to set new goals for himself, and it taught him a great deal about the complexities of producing an album.

With the failure of *Velvet Gloves and Spit,* Neil began to wonder whether he was going to have a future with Uni. But success eventually followed. Neil's single, "Brother Love's Traveling Salvation Show," a song heavily influenced by the gospel sound, established him as a star. It was the first song of what were later called his "theater pieces." These also included "Holly Holy" and "Soolaimon."

A friend introduced him to a record of an African tribal Mass, and Neil was totally caught up by it. He soon began collecting every type of African music he could find. The strange rhythms of African music took Neil's music in a new direction. It was a sound which accomplished what he was trying to do with Gospel.

Neil began by trying to write one song that would express all the feelings and love he had for African music. That was "Soolaimon." As he was writing and trying to record it, he realized that four minutes was not going to be nearly enough. So the one song grew into the "African Trilogy."

The "Trilogy," which is really six numbers instead of three, is what Neil calls a folk ballet. He used African beats, which were more sophisticated than African melodies, to depict the three principal stages in man's life — childhood, young adulthood, and old age. He chose African sounds because of his deep interest in gospel music and his desire to explore its rhythmic roots. Explore he did with a great deal of variety, from the toe-tapping "Soolaimon" to the tender, mystic "Childsong."

After some hesitation and fear of giving up a successful formula, Neil finally decided to record the "African Trilogy." He was ready to try something completely different. Neil recorded the album, *Tap Root Manuscript,* which highlighted "African Trilogy." It soon became a landmark album of 1970.

As a pop artist, Neil had enjoyed a long and steady ride on the charts, but he still felt hemmed in by his own style of music. He felt that he was not taken as seriously by critics as he would have liked. The "African Trilogy" quickly changed that.

Soon after *Tap Roots Manuscript* was released, Neil Diamond again astounded the music industry. He had eighteen months to go on his Universal contract, when it was announced that he would join Columbia Records. There he contracted for five years and five albums, guaranteeing him $1 million per album. People were astonished at the amount of money, which was then the most ever paid to an artist.

They were also surprised at the long term contract. The record industry is a business where the public's taste can be fickle and where acceptance can turn to indifference almost overnight. Yet one of the biggest, most important record companies was willing to gamble a fortune on Neil Diamond's power to last. This contract contained an even sweeter note for Neil because he had been signed briefly by Columbia almost a decade earlier, and had been dropped soon afterwards.

Movie Music

Columbia's faith in Neil Diamond was more than repaid when his first album was released. It was the original film soundtrack score for "Jonathan Livingston Seagull," based on the best-selling novel by Richard Bach. Neil was given the rare opportunity to create an hour's musical accompaniment for a motion picture which used no human beings, only animals and magnificent natural settings.

When Neil Diamond was first asked to compose the sound track for "Jonathan Livingston Seagull," he turned the offer down. His first reaction was, "Oh my God, what are they going to do? Are they going to make it in animation, making the birds move, their mouths move? Are there going to be humans in it?" But then he began to think about Jonathan and imagine what he would do with the score, and he found himself involved.

Neil identified very closely with Jonathan. He began to see himself in the gull's defeats and triumphs, and he started to believe in his philosophy. And, when he saw twenty minutes of the film which used some of the most spectacular photography he'd ever seen, he understood what he had to do. Neil knew he had to write the most beautiful music he could, music that would expand the story.

Neil went into his preparation with a passion. He studied film scoring. He reread Kahil Gibran's *The Prophet.* He collected books on philosophy to build up his vocabulary. He wanted to approach this writing more

18

carefully than he had ever done anything before. He had to decide on the type of language, on the attitude, and on the placement of the songs.

Neil's time and efforts were well-spent. As a result of his intense involvement in the story and the songs, the album became his second all-time bestseller. It was an immense hit abroad, even though the film was not well received. In 1973, "Jonathan Livingston Seagull" earned him a Grammy from the National Association of Recording Arts and Sciences and became the largest selling original sound track album in history. In addition, the Hollywood Foreign Press Association presented him with its Golden Globe Award for the sound track.

The Man Behind the Songs

Although most people find it hard to separate a Neil Diamond song from a Neil Diamond performance of that song, many of the world's most famous performers have recorded Neil's work. The list includes people from Elvis Presley to Arthur Fiedler and the Boston Pops. The reason his music is so popular and so often recorded is that Neil Diamond writes about human feelings which everyone has experienced. He writes about human beings, their weaknesses, their dreams, and their loneliness. He realizes that everybody knows a "song sung blue."

Neil is a person who is basically private and doesn't like to be interviewed. He avoids the spotlight of public attention. He reveals a lot about himself in his music. His songs have always meant the same thing for him. They have been a way to release his feelings, to say all the things he held in, all the words he couldn't say as a child. He is honest and open in his songs. Earlier, Neil's music had been a release for all kinds of feelings he didn't understand. Now music has an even broader meaning, and Neil not only needs it, he loves it. He is always plugged into his music.

The fact that Neil's music has been so successful probably indicates that many people feel as he does. Many seem to identify with the disappointments in "Solitary Man," the childhood loneliness of "Shilo," the joy and celebration of "Sweet Caroline," the search for one's self in "I Am . . . I Said," and the need for romance in "Play Me."

Neil's music shows the influence of many sounds. He borrows from the Latin dance bands he saw around New York, from the early, country-rooted records of such artists as the Everly Brothers and Roy Orbison, from the rock of his teenage years, from black gospel music and from African rhythms. Neil calls his music "urban rock 'n roll" because it combines all these different forms of city music.

Most of his melodies are filled with drama, and the lyrics are easily understood. Nevertheless, the lyrics take a long time to write. As Neil once said, "You have an attitude, a point to make in a very short time. You have to do it in a rhyming pattern you establish within the melody." The very personal song "I Am . . . I Said" took four months of work before Neil was satisfied that the words said what he actually felt. Before a song is written, recorded, and

21

performed, Neil has probably heard it in his head six or seven hundred times.

Neil once described his music: "Put the influences of my life, the music I've been exposed to, what I am as a person, and my needs into a pressure cooker called New York City. Let it simmer for about sixteen years and then take off the top. That explosion has lasted for fifteen years and will probably last until I die. Music is my voice."

On Tour

In the spring and early summer of 1972, Neil Diamond toured Great Britain and Western Europe. At every stop, he sang to enthusiastic audiences. His reception was fantastic. Reviewers praised the concerts. Audiences would stand and clap until he would come back for one more song. People would wait at the stage door to get a closer look at him. The feeling of the lonely boy turned out to be the feeling of the world, and his sound was the music hidden in all people.

On Thursday, August 24, 1972, Neil Diamond was back in the United States. it was a hot summer night in California, where they call it "earthquake weather." It could very well have been a scene from "Brother Love's Traveling Salvation Show" with "the leaves hanging down and the grass on the ground smelling sweet."

The air hung heavy over the open shell of the Greek Theatre and the 4,500 people in it. Climbing up the mountain and into the surrounding trees were countless other people who were unable to get a prized ticket. They would do anything to have a glimpse of the stage and the man who would fill it. Many of the people had been there on Tuesday and Wednesday and would be there again on Friday and the nights after that, because Neil Diamond had come back to the Greek.

Softly, the music began and the lights dimmed. Neil Diamond emerged from a dramatic puff of steam to the rocking beat of a six-piece band. There he stood, as if it were the most natural thing in the world for those people to be demanding a bit of his soul. A battery of spotlights picked out his long black hair and pale features, set off by scarlet slacks and a gold embroidered shirt. "We're all strangers here," Neil told his hypnotized listeners. "We're in a great theater decorated in red and gold, but none of it means a thing if we don't get it off together. I want my music to move you and to touch you." And when he slipped into the familiar lyrics of "Solitary Man," his earliest success, the crowd roared its approval.

For the next 107 minutes, he gave them his music, a spontaneous and exhausting display of energy and feeling. The people were right there with him, screaming and cheering and applauding. They knew all the words to all the songs, but they were hearing them as though for the first time. That's what Neil Diamond gives to the people at his concerts. He sings as though he, too, were just discovering the heart and soul of the music. He makes every number unique and exciting.

Neil Diamond's concert at the Greek Theatre is typical of what makes him a dynamic concert attraction. He is a total performer before a live audience with whom he seems to create an instant friendship.

As Robert Hilburn, Pop Music Critic for the *Los Angeles Times,* wrote: "Shunning the usual concert musts and samenesses, Diamond's performance is a virtual model for an entertainer who wants to make a personal, distinctive musical statement."

Hilburn added, "Most of all, he gives of himself. All too often, major pop music figures seem to approach a concert as if they are going on stage to take bows for what they've already done on record. Diamond, however, wisely thinks of a concert in a different, more productive light. From care in production to intensity of his own performance, he takes advantage of the live encounter with his audience to prove he is even better than you thought he was."

The Greek Theatre appearance set an all-time box office record for a ten-performance engagement. Neil's memorable concert there was recorded "live" and became the biggest selling album hit of his career — "Hot August Night." The double album again showed how far across the world Neil Diamond's popularity had spread. It became his largest selling album in every country in which it was released. In Australia, it became the biggest selling album in history. It remained in the number one spot on the hit charts for twenty-six weeks and was the first album ever to produce more than $2 million in sales. It was finally forced from the number one spot by another Diamond album, "Jonathan Livingston Seagull."

Following his performance at the Greek, Neil played a series of concert dates in places where he had never performed before. The highlight of this "mini-tour" was his two-night stand at the original Grand Ole Opry House in Nashville.

Then Neil took on what was to become an historic engagement: The Schubert Organization presented him in concert for a twenty performance one-man-show at its Winter Garden Theater in New York City. This made Neil the first pop-rock superstar to "headline" on Broadway.

On the surface it seemed to be a hasty and reckless idea. One-man shows have traditionally been associated with superstar talents like Judy Garland and Danny Kaye. There hadn't been a one-man show at the Winter Garden since the 1930's. Jose Feliciano's similar attempt on Broadway the month before had been unsuccessful. Neil was certainly taking a chance.

Opening night on Broadway, October 5, 1972, was a night Neil Diamond will remember forever. A critic from *The New York Times* hailed it as "an idea whose time had come . . . the right performer in the right circumstances . . . the final stage in the mass popularization of rock." The *Times* also volunteered that Neil's "performance was not only a personal triumph for him, but also a small stimulus in a show business development that may start a few vital juices flowing in that tired old lady, Broadway."

Winter Garden was an uncertain chance to take, but Neil Diamond is an adventurous young man who enjoys challenges. He had both the musical ability and the stage presence to carry off the performance. He didn't have to worry about comparisons with the likes of Judy Garland and Danny Kaye. His command of the stage, his timing, and his self-confidence were superb. Because the Winter Garden engagement was such a success, Neil became the trailblazer for a small army of other pop stars who have followed in his footsteps.

26

A Time for Quiet

By 1973, with several successful years of performing behind him, Neil Diamond had become a superstar. Only the Beatles could match his record of eleven best-selling albums, and the twelfth was already past the million dollar mark before it was even released. Since his hit, "Solitary Man" in 1966, there seemed to be an endless flow of songs such as "Cherry, Cherry," "Sweet Caroline," "Holly Holy," "Song Sung Blue." By 1972, he had earned more than 5 million dollars.

Neil's fans were astounded, then, when he announced his retirement from the concert stage for a year, or probably two. It was assumed that he was suffering from fatigue and would soon forget his promise to return, as had scores of other artists.

But what the public did not take into consideration was that Neil's plan was well thought out. Neil simply wanted time to wind down, to think, to study, to read, and to write uninterruptedly. He wanted some time to try classical piano and guitar and to learn how to compose for string quartets. He hoped, too, to discover new ways of expressing his ideas in music and new ways of performing. He wanted to set new goals for himself so that he might maintain his enthusiasm for his work. He wanted to be able to spend more time with his wife, Marcia, and their son, Jesse.

As Neil once described his plan, "I want some time off. I want to study piano. I want to learn the technical language of music so I can better communicate with musicians. I want time to read, to explore myself and the things around me. I've been collecting books for two years, looking forward to the time I could sit down and read

them. But things have been too busy, too tense to allow it.''

Neil knew this step was a risk. But it had been daring for Neil to move to the UNI Record label and attempt songs that were more personal in expression and more sophisticated in design. It had been a challenge for him to be the first solo performer to play the Winter Garden Theater since Al Jolson in the 1930's. So he was used to taking chances. And Neil takes a long view of his career. As he once said, ''I'd like to think I can keep myself excited and enthused for as long as I live. I'd like to think I have twenty or thirty more productive years. That's what I dream about.''

Neil closed one chapter in his life by taking a leave from performing, and he began another in quiet study. It was Neil's hope that by exploring his own feelings, he would be able to give his fans more in the future. There was a large audience waiting for his return.

Neil Diamond actively reclaimed his territory in 1974. That year he released a new album, ''Neil Diamond/Serenade,'' and he announced his planned return to the concert stage.

Return

In ''Serenade,'' he returned to a type of music in which he excels. It is a collection of separate songs without any connecting theme, songs he *had* to write at the very moment they were created inside his mind. They are songs of varying styles, rhythms, lengths, and moods.

As he returned to the spotlight, Neil found that his audience was still as large and as varied as the one which had bid him farewell a year before, the one that had supported him for almost a decade. This audience continued to exist, even in his absence, because Neil Diamond had never taken them for granted.

His return to the concert world after a long absence is now being plotted as a series of independent mini-tours in various parts of the world, separated by lay-off periods in which he will return to the recording studio. This plan will take about eighteen months to complete.

The coming seasons will also see Neil's long-awaited debut on television and perhaps in motion pictures. He has said this will happen "When the time and project are right."

Neil Diamond is unique. His musical passion, creativity, and continual growth seem to know no limits, no permanency, no pattern. He firmly believes that to stay in the same place musically is the same as slipping backwards. Neil thinks an artist should constantly change, grow, and mature.

Today, Neil Diamond has matured into a smooth, inventive composer-performer. His various talents have enabled him to grow from a singer of pop songs to a superstar. The frog has become a king.

JACKSON FIVE   NEIL DIAMOND
CARLY SIMON   CAROLE KING
BOB DYLAN   DIANA ROSS
JOHN DENVER   THE OSMONDS
THE BEATLES   CHARLIE RICH
ELVIS PRESLEY   ELTON JOHN
JOHNNY CASH   CHICAGO
CHARLEY PRIDE   FRANK SINATRA
ARETHA FRANKLIN   BARBRA STREISAND
ROBERTA FLACK   OLIVIA NEWTON-JOHN
STEVIE WONDER

Rock'n
PopStars